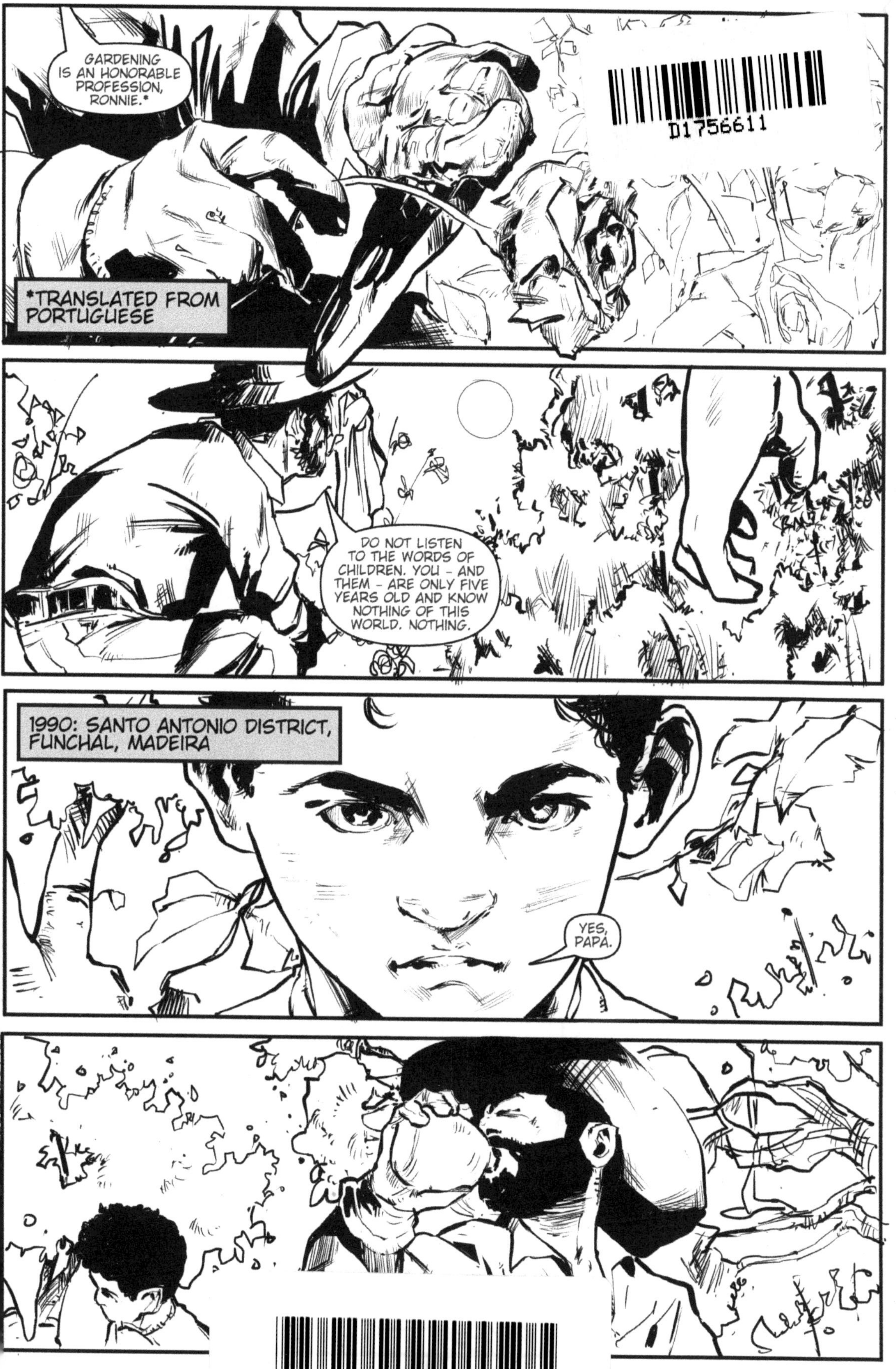
GARDENING IS AN HONORABLE PROFESSION, RONNIE.*
*TRANSLATED FROM PORTUGUESE
DO NOT LISTEN TO THE WORDS OF CHILDREN. YOU - AND THEM - ARE ONLY FIVE YEARS OLD AND KNOW NOTHING OF THIS WORLD. NOTHING.
1990: SANTO ANTONIO DISTRICT, FUNCHAL, MADEIRA
YES, PAPA.

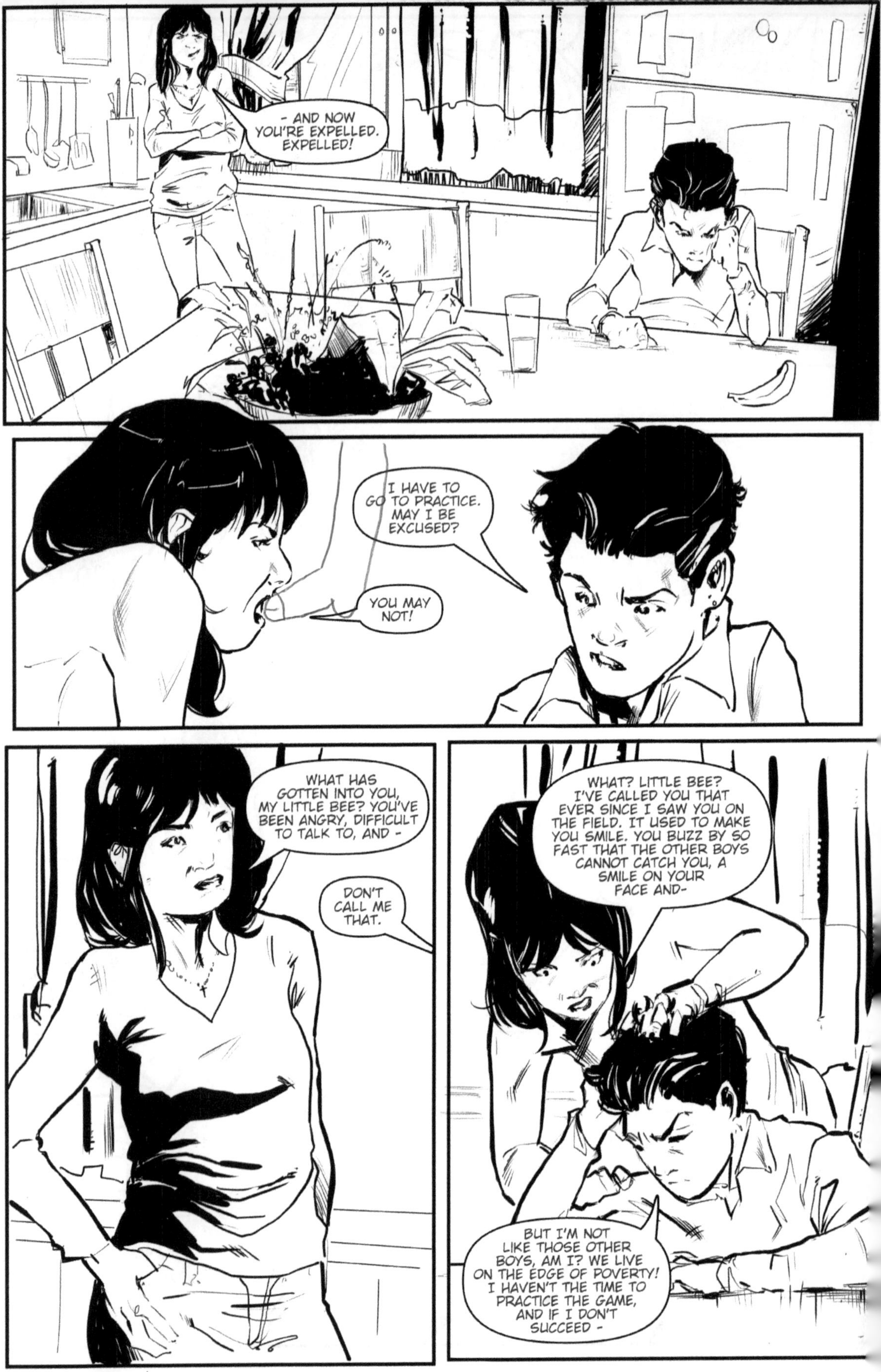
- AND NOW YOU'RE EXPELLED. EXPELLED!
I HAVE TO GO TO PRACTICE. MAY I BE EXCUSED?
YOU MAY NOT!
WHAT HAS GOTTEN INTO YOU, MY LITTLE BEE? YOU'VE BEEN ANGRY, DIFFICULT TO TALK TO, AND -
DON'T CALL ME THAT.
WHAT? LITTLE BEE? I'VE CALLED YOU THAT EVER SINCE I SAW YOU ON THE FIELD. IT USED TO MAKE YOU SMILE. YOU BUZZ BY SO FAST THAT THE OTHER BOYS CANNOT CATCH YOU, A SMILE ON YOUR FACE AND-
BUT I'M NOT LIKE THOSE OTHER BOYS, AM I? WE LIVE ON THE EDGE OF POVERTY! I HAVEN'T THE TIME TO PRACTICE THE GAME, AND IF I DON'T SUCCEED -

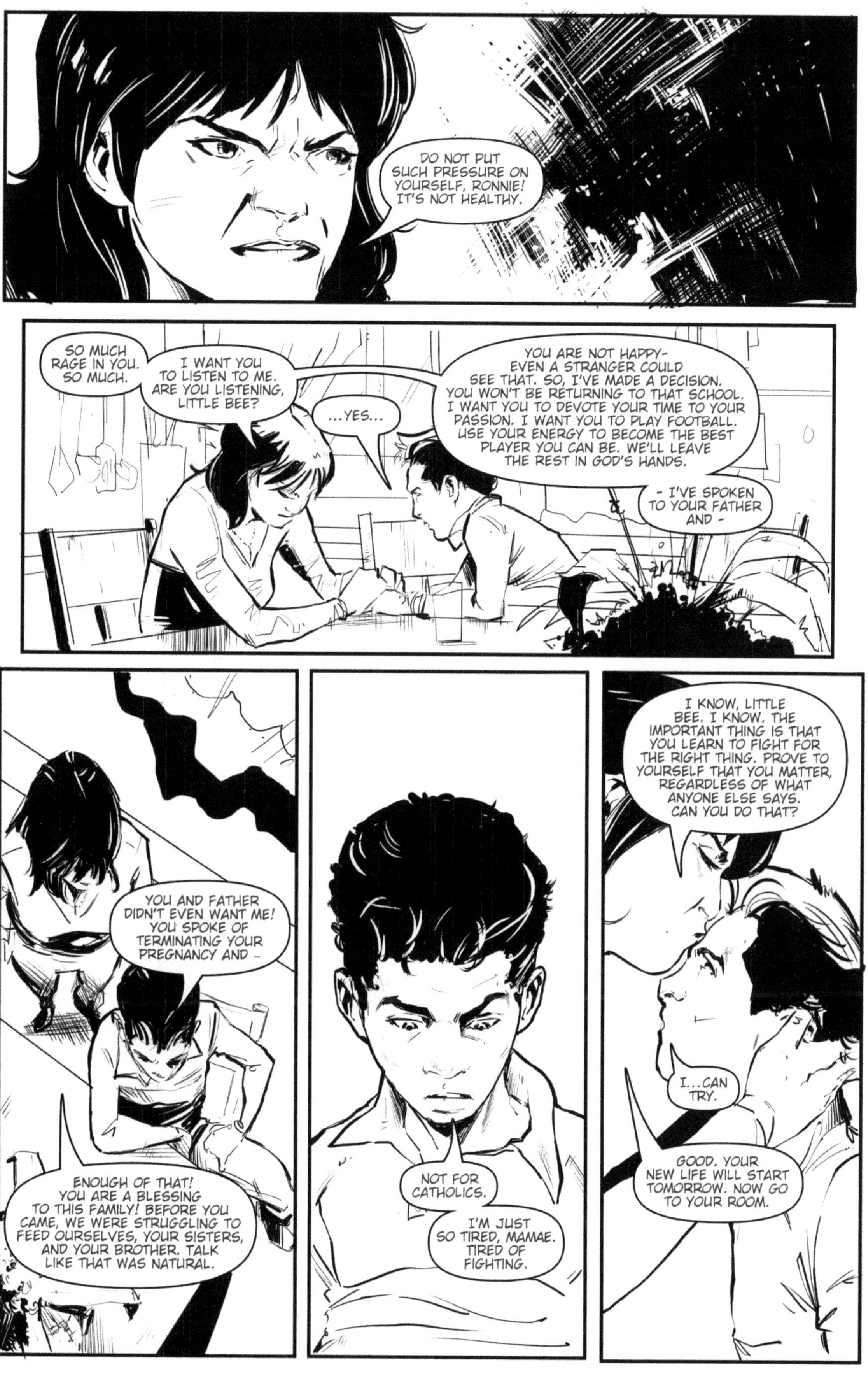
DO NOT PUT SUCH PRESSURE ON YOURSELF, RONNIE! IT'S NOT HEALTHY.
SO MUCH RAGE IN YOU. SO MUCH.
I WANT YOU TO LISTEN TO ME. ARE YOU LISTENING, LITTLE BEE?
...YES...
YOU ARE NOT HAPPY- EVEN A STRANGER COULD SEE THAT. SO, I'VE MADE A DECISION. YOU WON'T BE RETURNING TO THAT SCHOOL. I WANT YOU TO DEVOTE YOUR TIME TO YOUR PASSION. I WANT YOU TO PLAY FOOTBALL. USE YOUR ENERGY TO BECOME THE BEST PLAYER YOU CAN BE. WE'LL LEAVE THE REST IN GOD'S HANDS.
- I'VE SPOKEN TO YOUR FATHER AND -
YOU AND FATHER DIDN'T EVEN WANT ME! YOU SPOKE OF TERMINATING YOUR PREGNANCY AND -
ENOUGH OF THAT! YOU ARE A BLESSING TO THIS FAMILY! BEFORE YOU CAME, WE WERE STRUGGLING TO FEED OURSELVES, YOUR SISTERS, AND YOUR BROTHER. TALK LIKE THAT WAS NATURAL.
NOT FOR CATHOLICS.
I'M JUST SO TIRED, MAMAE. TIRED OF FIGHTING.
I KNOW, LITTLE BEE. I KNOW. THE IMPORTANT THING IS THAT YOU LEARN TO FIGHT FOR THE RIGHT THING. PROVE TO YOURSELF THAT YOU MATTER, REGARDLESS OF WHAT ANYONE ELSE SAYS. CAN YOU DO THAT?
I...CAN TRY.
GOOD. YOUR NEW LIFE WILL START TOMORROW. NOW GO TO YOUR ROOM.

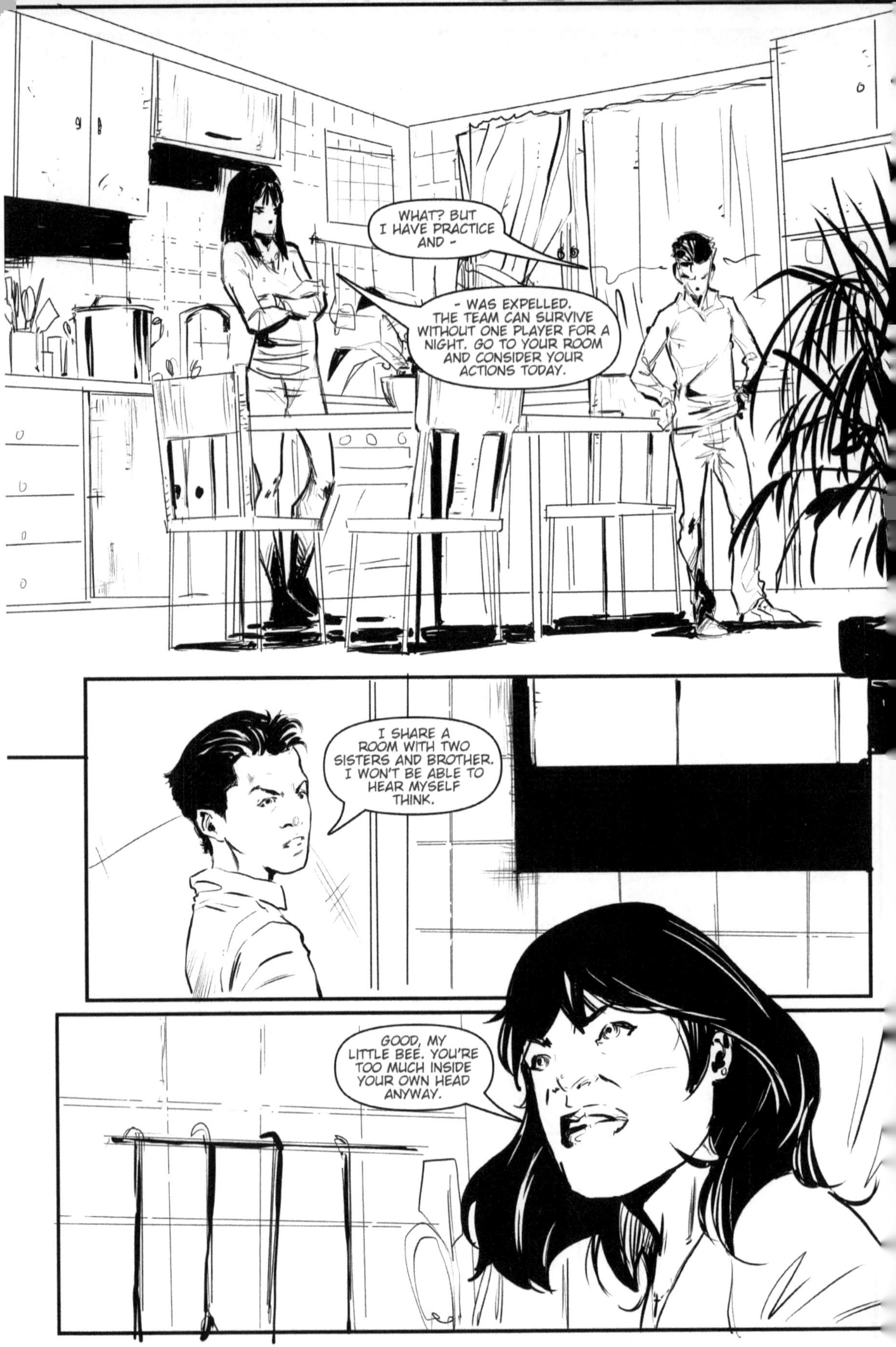
WHAT? BUT I HAVE PRACTICE AND -
- WAS EXPELLED. THE TEAM CAN SURVIVE WITHOUT ONE PLAYER FOR A NIGHT. GO TO YOUR ROOM AND CONSIDER YOUR ACTIONS TODAY.
I SHARE A ROOM WITH TWO SISTERS AND BROTHER. I WON'T BE ABLE TO HEAR MYSELF THINK.
GOOD, MY LITTLE BEE. YOU'RE TOO MUCH INSIDE YOUR OWN HEAD ANYWAY.

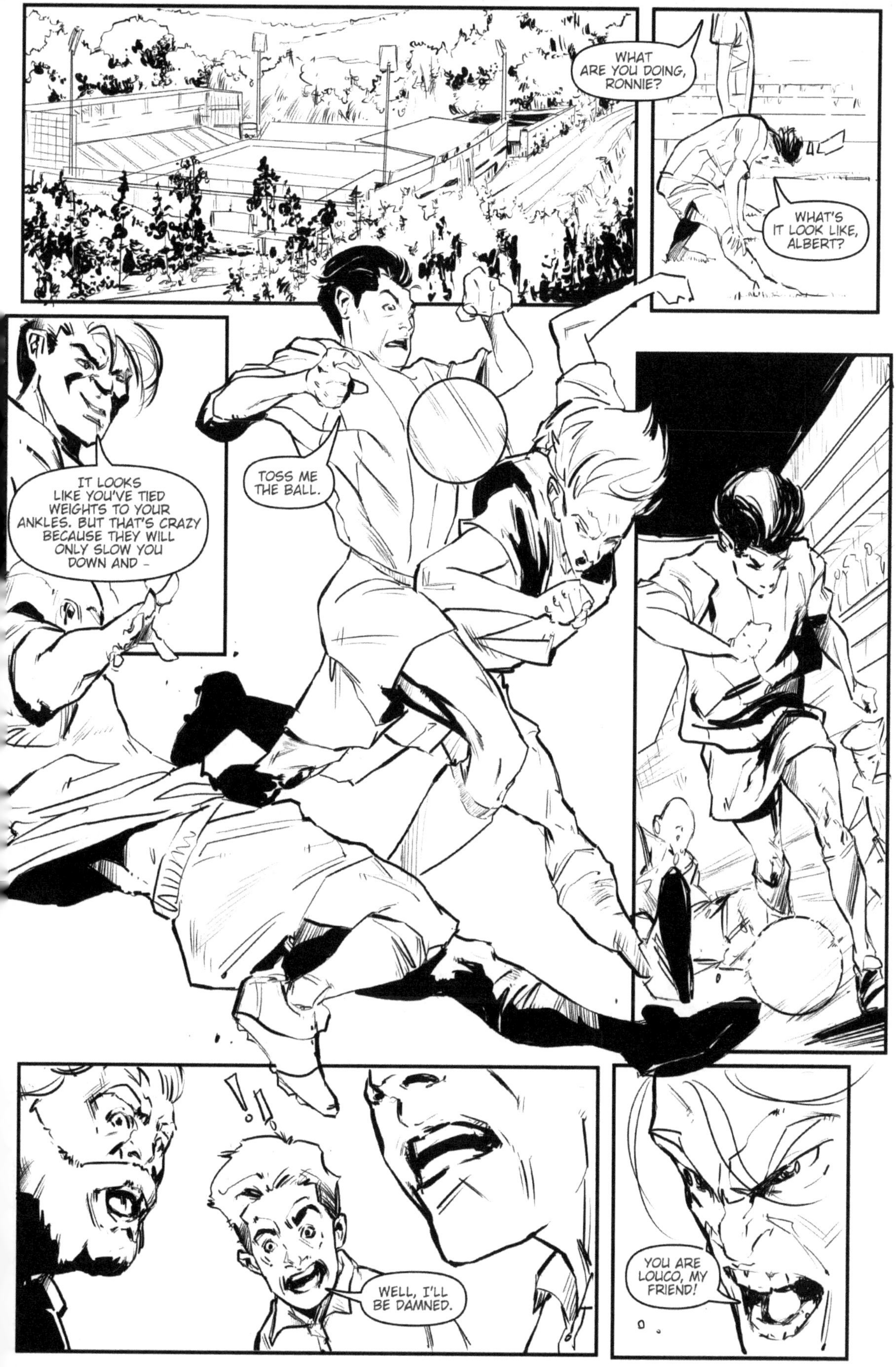
WHAT ARE YOU DOING, RONNIE?
WHAT'S IT LOOK LIKE, ALBERT?
IT LOOKS LIKE YOU'VE TIED WEIGHTS TO YOUR ANKLES. BUT THAT'S CRAZY BECAUSE THEY WILL ONLY SLOW YOU DOWN AND -
TOSS ME THE BALL.
!!
WELL, I'LL BE DAMNED.
YOU ARE LOUCO, MY FRIEND!

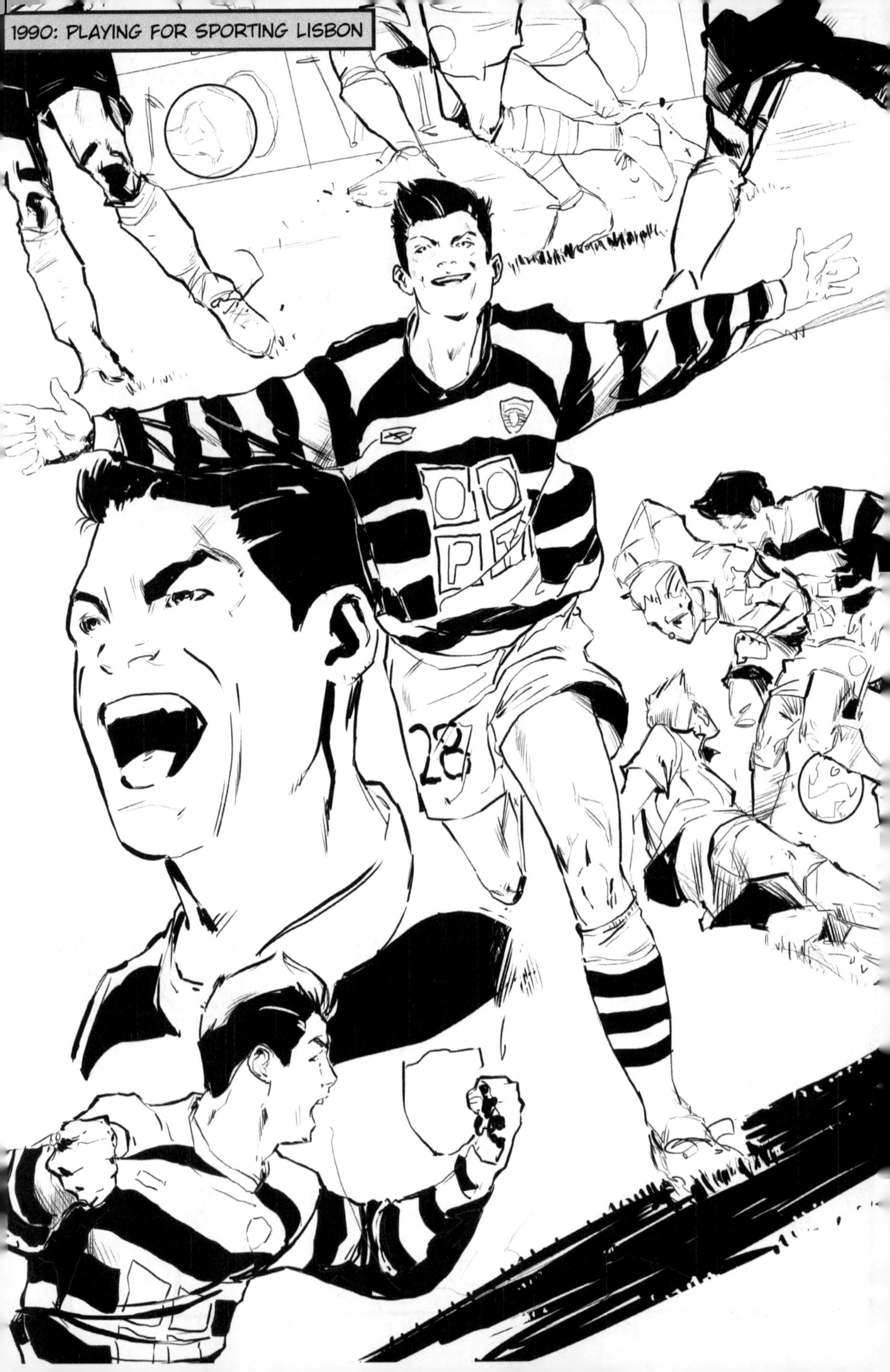
1990: PLAYING FOR SPORTING LISBON

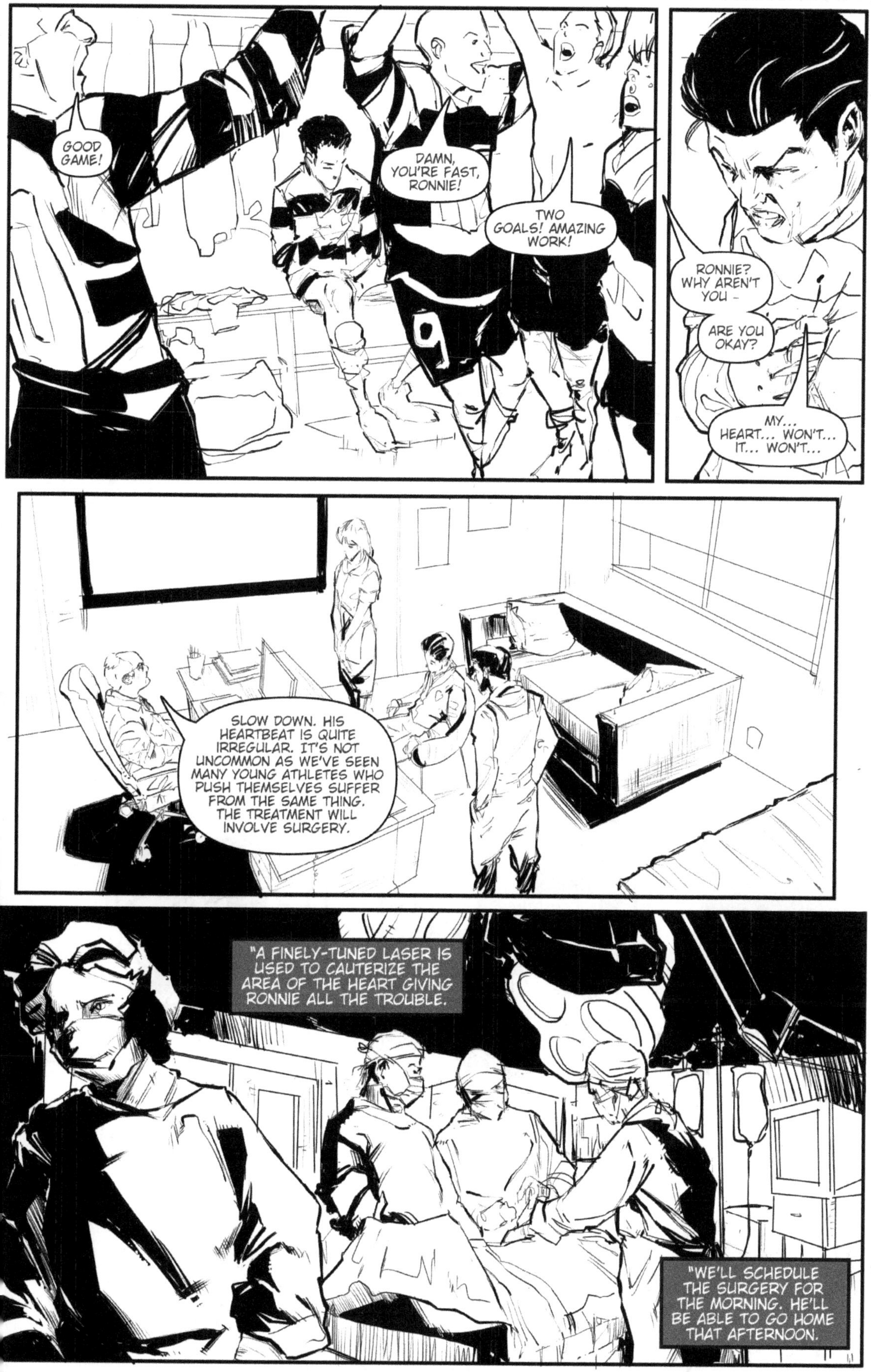
GOOD GAME!
DAMN, YOU'RE FAST, RONNIE!
TWO GOALS! AMAZING WORK!
RONNIE? WHY AREN'T YOU -
ARE YOU OKAY?
MY... HEART... WON'T... IT... WON'T...
SLOW DOWN. HIS HEARTBEAT IS QUITE IRREGULAR. IT'S NOT UNCOMMON AS WE'VE SEEN MANY YOUNG ATHLETES WHO PUSH THEMSELVES SUFFER FROM THE SAME THING. THE TREATMENT WILL INVOLVE SURGERY.
"A FINELY-TUNED LASER IS USED TO CAUTERIZE THE AREA OF THE HEART GIVING RONNIE ALL THE TROUBLE.
"WE'LL SCHEDULE THE SURGERY FOR THE MORNING. HE'LL BE ABLE TO GO HOME THAT AFTERNOON.

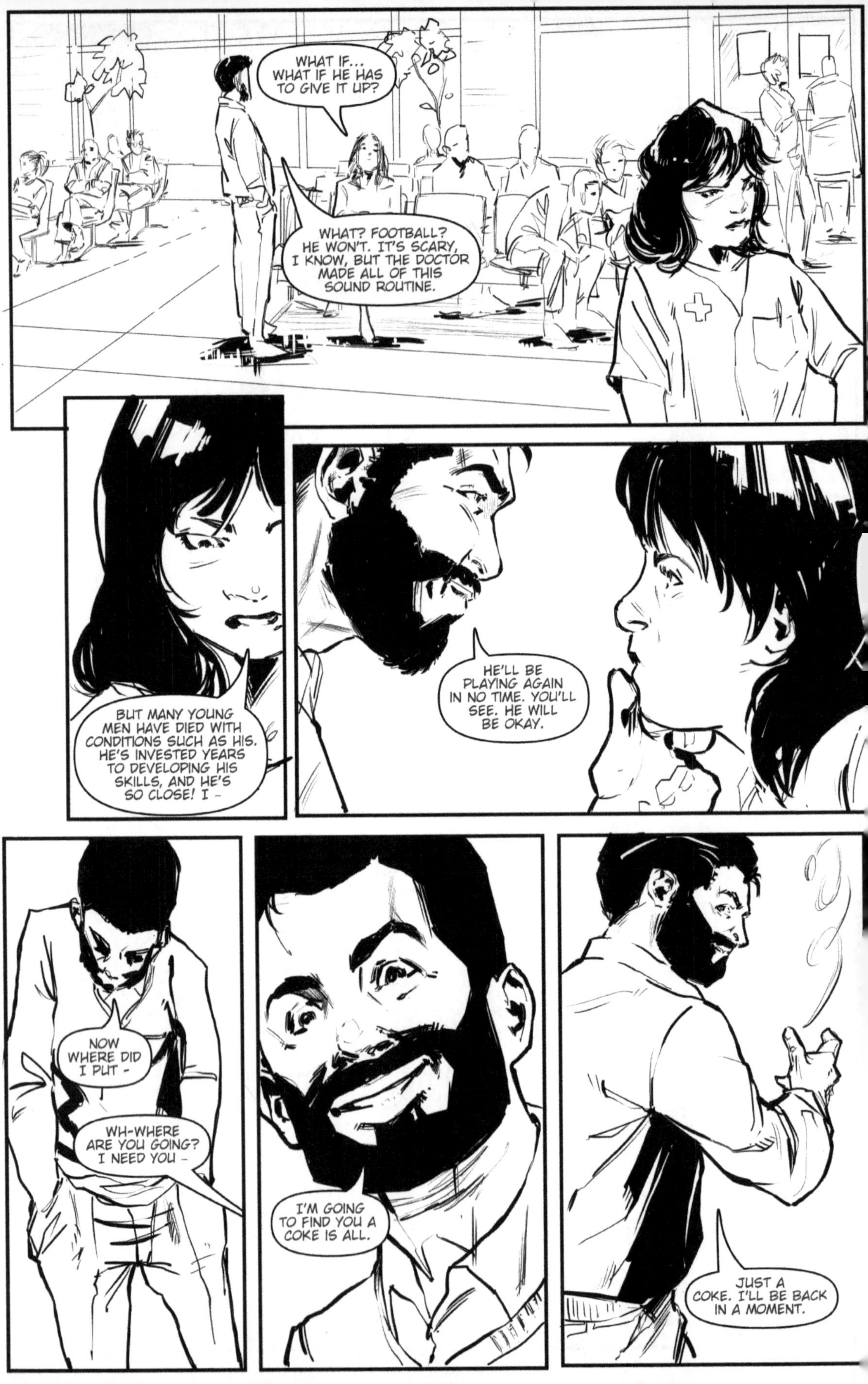
WHAT IF... WHAT IF HE HAS TO GIVE IT UP?
WHAT? FOOTBALL? HE WON'T. IT'S SCARY, I KNOW, BUT THE DOCTOR MADE ALL OF THIS SOUND ROUTINE.
BUT MANY YOUNG MEN HAVE DIED WITH CONDITIONS SUCH AS HIS. HE'S INVESTED YEARS TO DEVELOPING HIS SKILLS, AND HE'S SO CLOSE! I -
HE'LL BE PLAYING AGAIN IN NO TIME. YOU'LL SEE. HE WILL BE OKAY.
NOW WHERE DID I PUT -
WH-WHERE ARE YOU GOING? I NEED YOU -
I'M GOING TO FIND YOU A COKE IS ALL.
JUST A COKE. I'LL BE BACK IN A MOMENT.

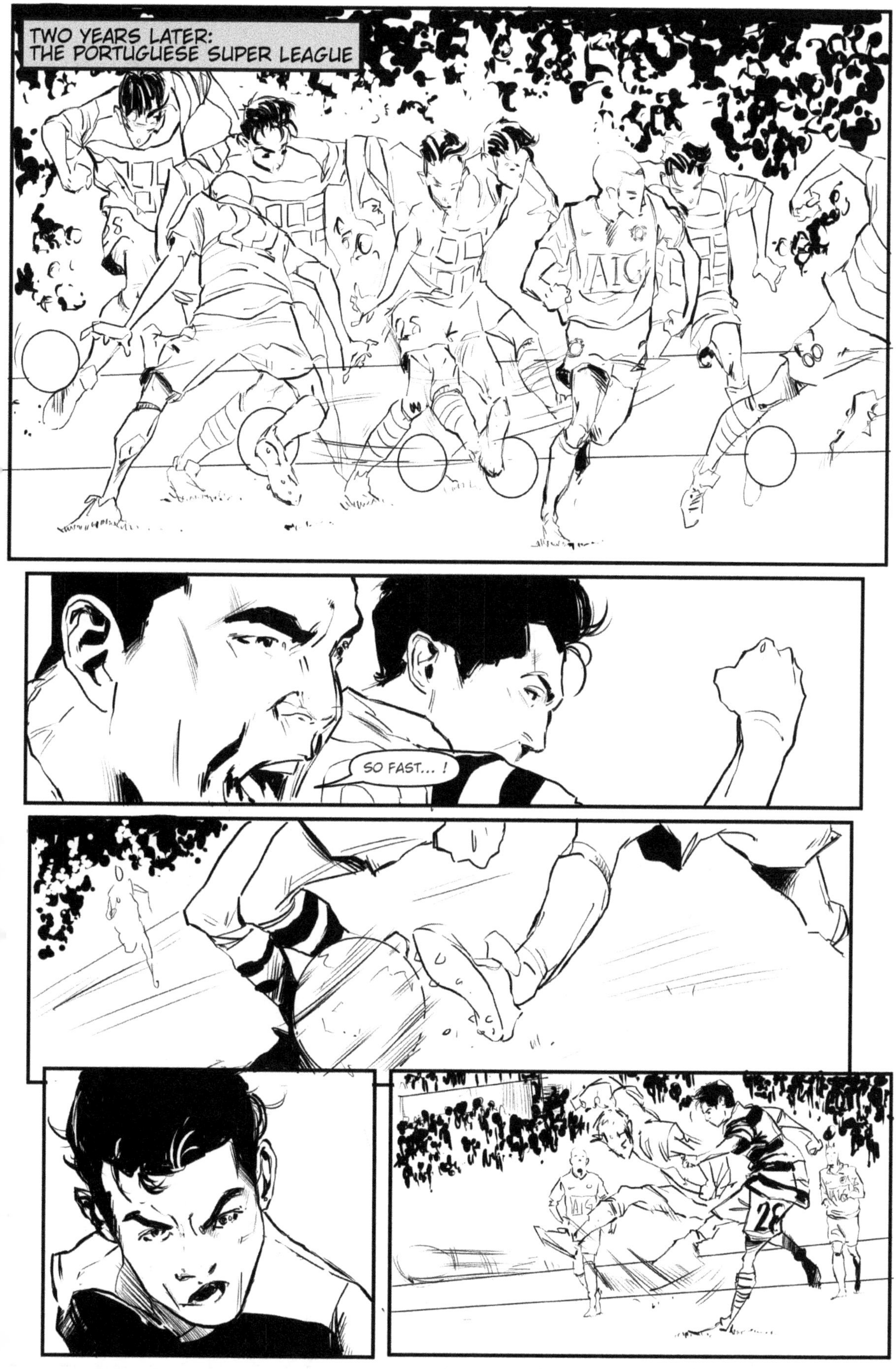
TWO YEARS LATER:
THE PORTUGUESE SUPER LEAGUE
SO FAST... !

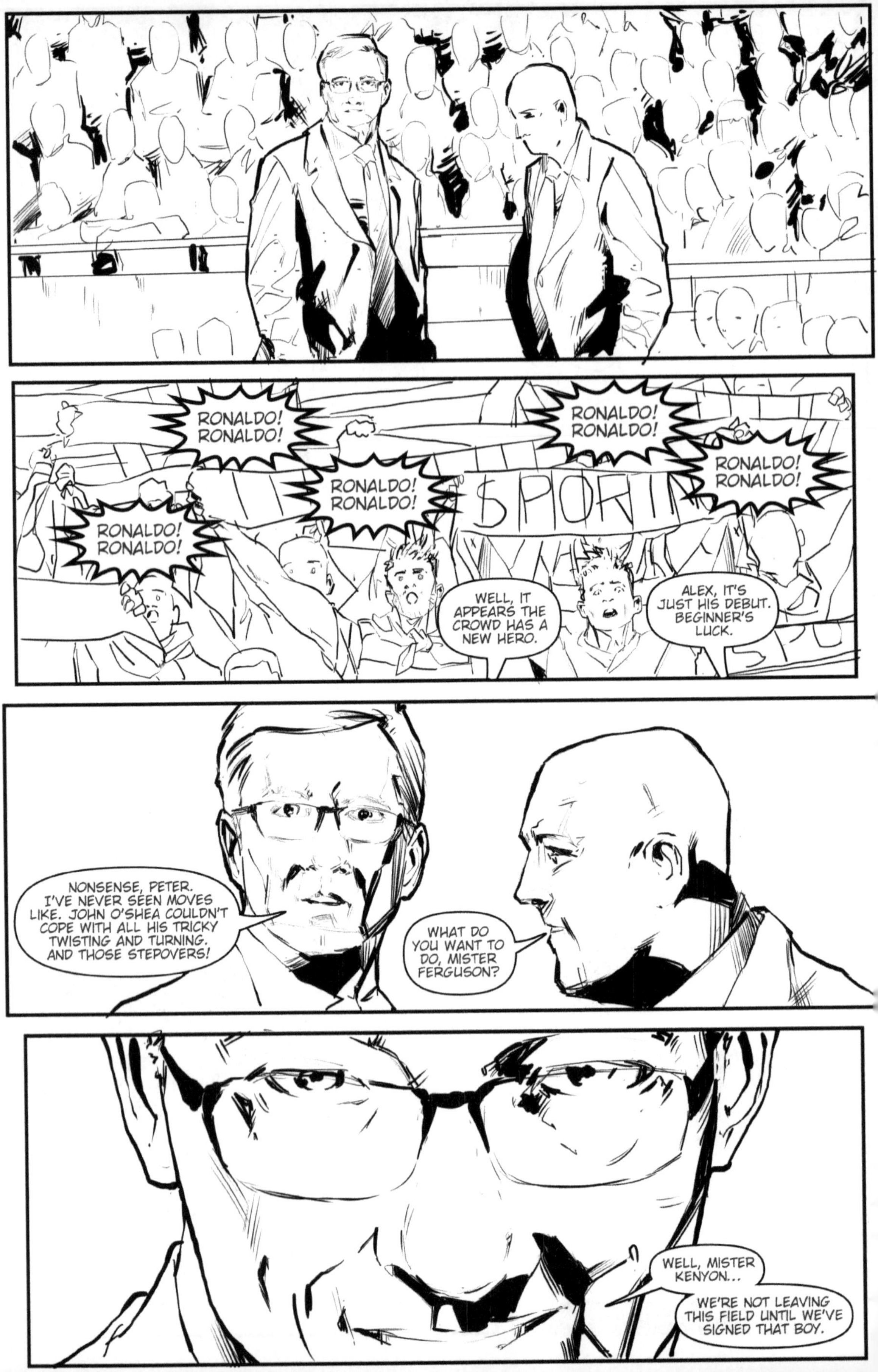
RONALDO! RONALDO!
RONALDO! RONALDO!
RONALDO! RONALDO!
RONALDO! RONALDO!
RONALDO! RONALDO!
SPORTI
WELL, IT APPEARS THE CROWD HAS A NEW HERO.
ALEX, IT'S JUST HIS DEBUT. BEGINNER'S LUCK.
NONSENSE, PETER. I'VE NEVER SEEN MOVES LIKE. JOHN O'SHEA COULDN'T COPE WITH ALL HIS TRICKY TWISTING AND TURNING. AND THOSE STEPOVERS!
WHAT DO YOU WANT TO DO, MISTER FERGUSON?
WELL, MISTER KENYON...
WE'RE NOT LEAVING THIS FIELD UNTIL WE'VE SIGNED THAT BOY.

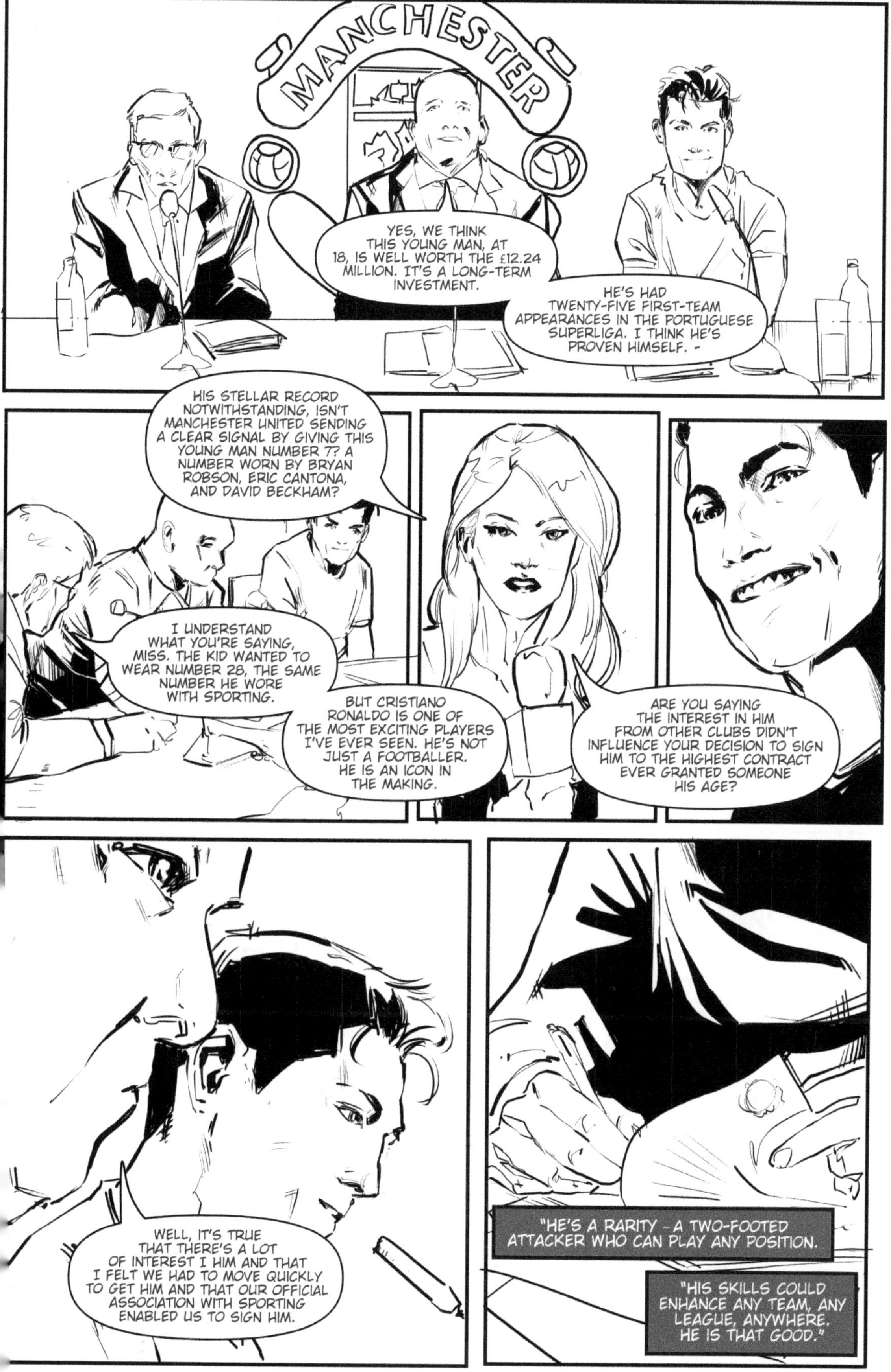
MANCHESTER
YES, WE THINK THIS YOUNG MAN, AT 18, IS WELL WORTH THE £12.24 MILLION. IT'S A LONG-TERM INVESTMENT.
HE'S HAD TWENTY-FIVE FIRST-TEAM APPEARANCES IN THE PORTUGUESE SUPERLIGA. I THINK HE'S PROVEN HIMSELF. -
HIS STELLAR RECORD NOTWITHSTANDING, ISN'T MANCHESTER UNITED SENDING A CLEAR SIGNAL BY GIVING THIS YOUNG MAN NUMBER 7? A NUMBER WORN BY BRYAN ROBSON, ERIC CANTONA, AND DAVID BECKHAM?
I UNDERSTAND WHAT YOU'RE SAYING, MISS. THE KID WANTED TO WEAR NUMBER 28, THE SAME NUMBER HE WORE WITH SPORTING.
BUT CRISTIANO RONALDO IS ONE OF THE MOST EXCITING PLAYERS I'VE EVER SEEN. HE'S NOT JUST A FOOTBALLER. HE IS AN ICON IN THE MAKING.
ARE YOU SAYING THE INTEREST IN HIM FROM OTHER CLUBS DIDN'T INFLUENCE YOUR DECISION TO SIGN HIM TO THE HIGHEST CONTRACT EVER GRANTED SOMEONE HIS AGE?
WELL, IT'S TRUE THAT THERE'S A LOT OF INTEREST I HIM AND THAT I FELT WE HAD TO MOVE QUICKLY TO GET HIM AND THAT OUR OFFICIAL ASSOCIATION WITH SPORTING ENABLED US TO SIGN HIM.
"HE'S A RARITY – A TWO-FOOTED ATTACKER WHO CAN PLAY ANY POSITION.
"HIS SKILLS COULD ENHANCE ANY TEAM, ANY LEAGUE, ANYWHERE. HE IS THAT GOOD."

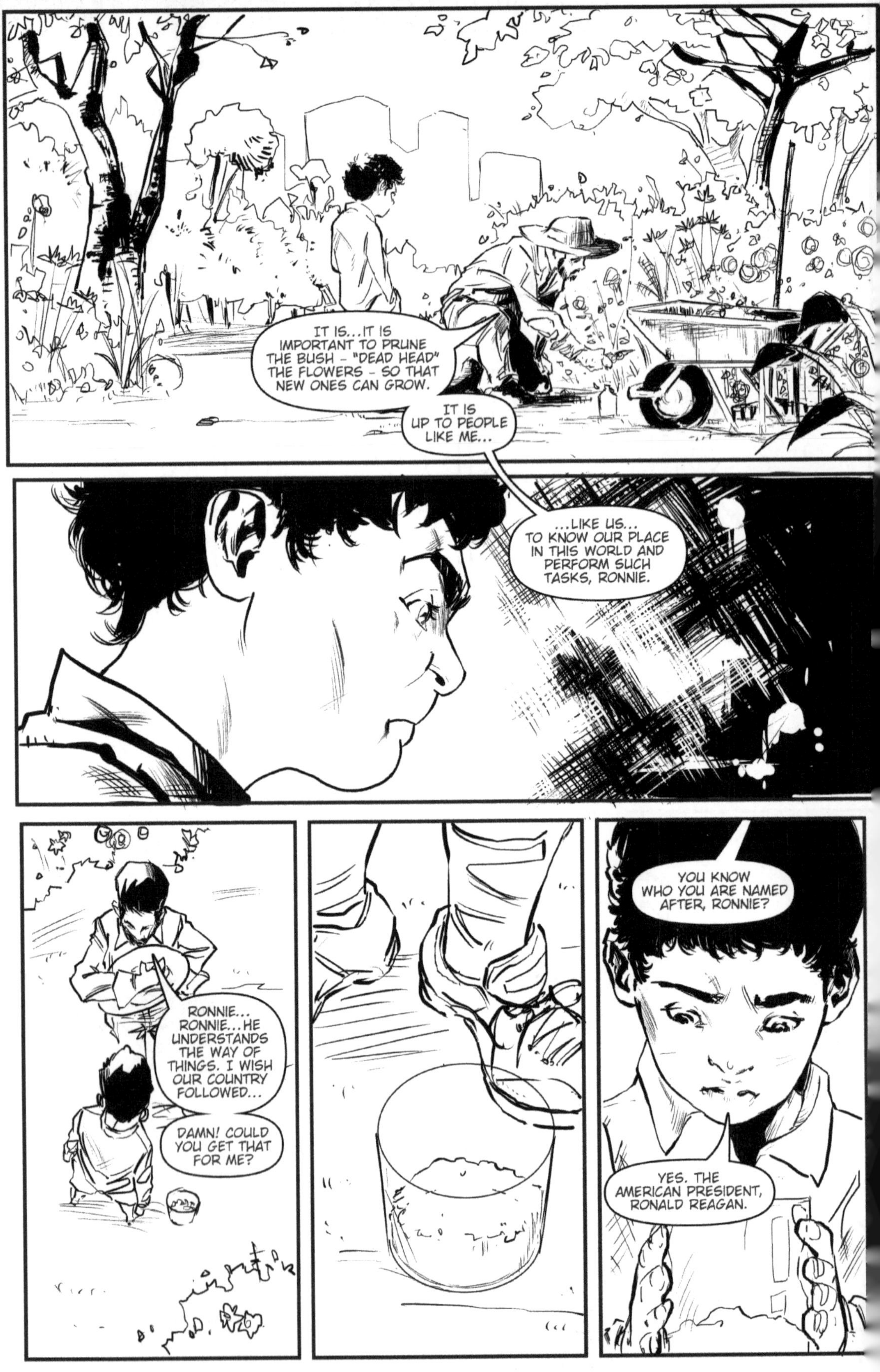
IT IS...IT IS IMPORTANT TO PRUNE THE BUSH - "DEAD HEAD" THE FLOWERS - SO THAT NEW ONES CAN GROW.
IT IS UP TO PEOPLE LIKE ME...
...LIKE US... TO KNOW OUR PLACE IN THIS WORLD AND PERFORM SUCH TASKS, RONNIE.
RONNIE... RONNIE...HE UNDERSTANDS THE WAY OF THINGS. I WISH OUR COUNTRY FOLLOWED...
DAMN! COULD YOU GET THAT FOR ME?
YOU KNOW WHO YOU ARE NAMED AFTER, RONNIE?
YES. THE AMERICAN PRESIDENT, RONALD REAGAN.

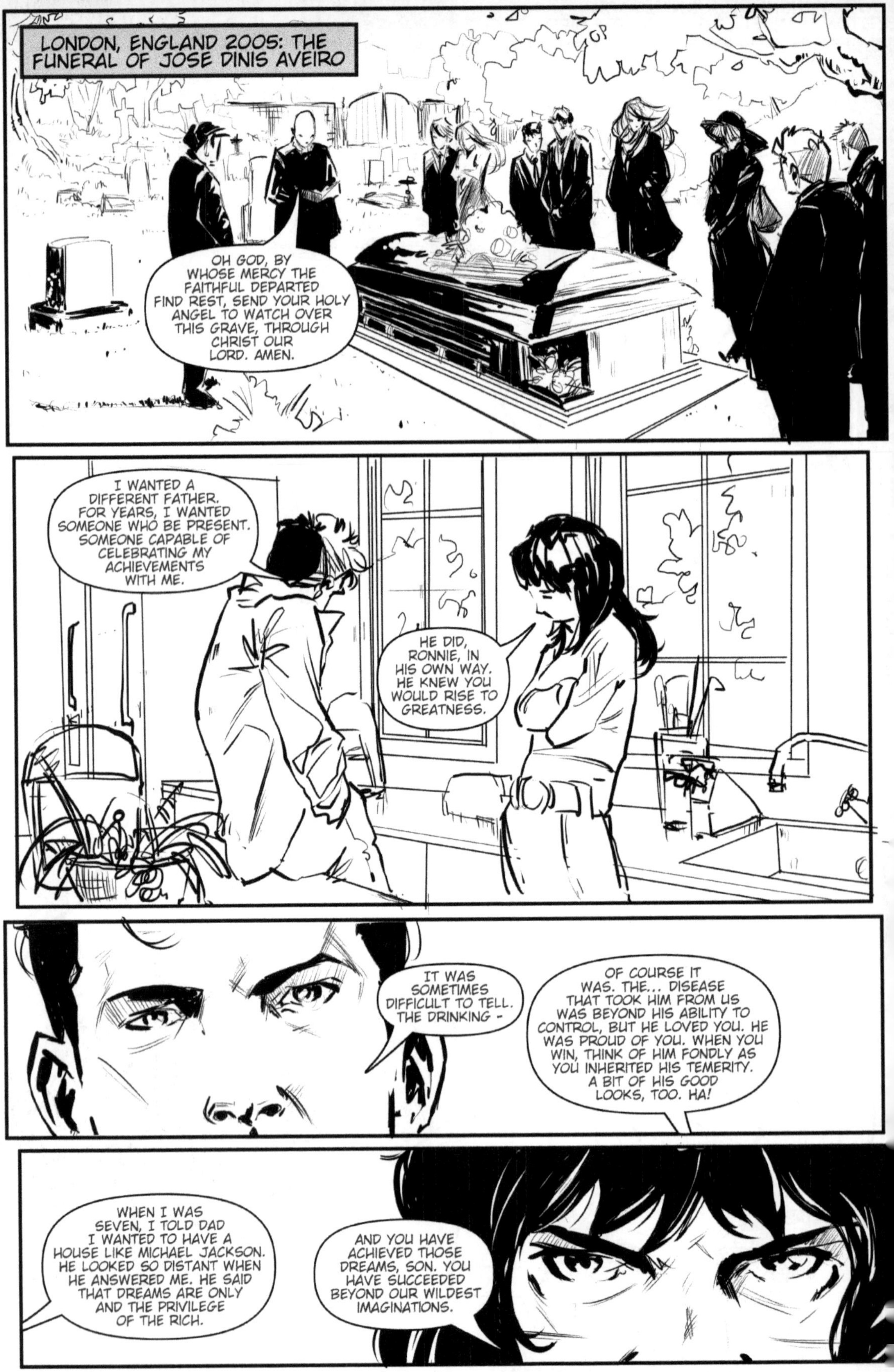
LONDON, ENGLAND 2005: THE FUNERAL OF JOSE DINIS AVEIRO
OH GOD, BY WHOSE MERCY THE FAITHFUL DEPARTED FIND REST, SEND YOUR HOLY ANGEL TO WATCH OVER THIS GRAVE, THROUGH CHRIST OUR LORD. AMEN.
I WANTED A DIFFERENT FATHER. FOR YEARS, I WANTED SOMEONE WHO BE PRESENT. SOMEONE CAPABLE OF CELEBRATING MY ACHIEVEMENTS WITH ME.
HE DID, RONNIE, IN HIS OWN WAY. HE KNEW YOU WOULD RISE TO GREATNESS.
IT WAS SOMETIMES DIFFICULT TO TELL. THE DRINKING -
OF COURSE IT WAS. THE... DISEASE THAT TOOK HIM FROM US WAS BEYOND HIS ABILITY TO CONTROL, BUT HE LOVED YOU. HE WAS PROUD OF YOU. WHEN YOU WIN, THINK OF HIM FONDLY AS YOU INHERITED HIS TEMERITY. A BIT OF HIS GOOD LOOKS, TOO. HA!
WHEN I WAS SEVEN, I TOLD DAD I WANTED TO HAVE A HOUSE LIKE MICHAEL JACKSON. HE LOOKED SO DISTANT WHEN HE ANSWERED ME. HE SAID THAT DREAMS ARE ONLY AND THE PRIVILEGE OF THE RICH.
AND YOU HAVE ACHIEVED THOSE DREAMS, SON. YOU HAVE SUCCEEDED BEYOND OUR WILDEST IMAGINATIONS.

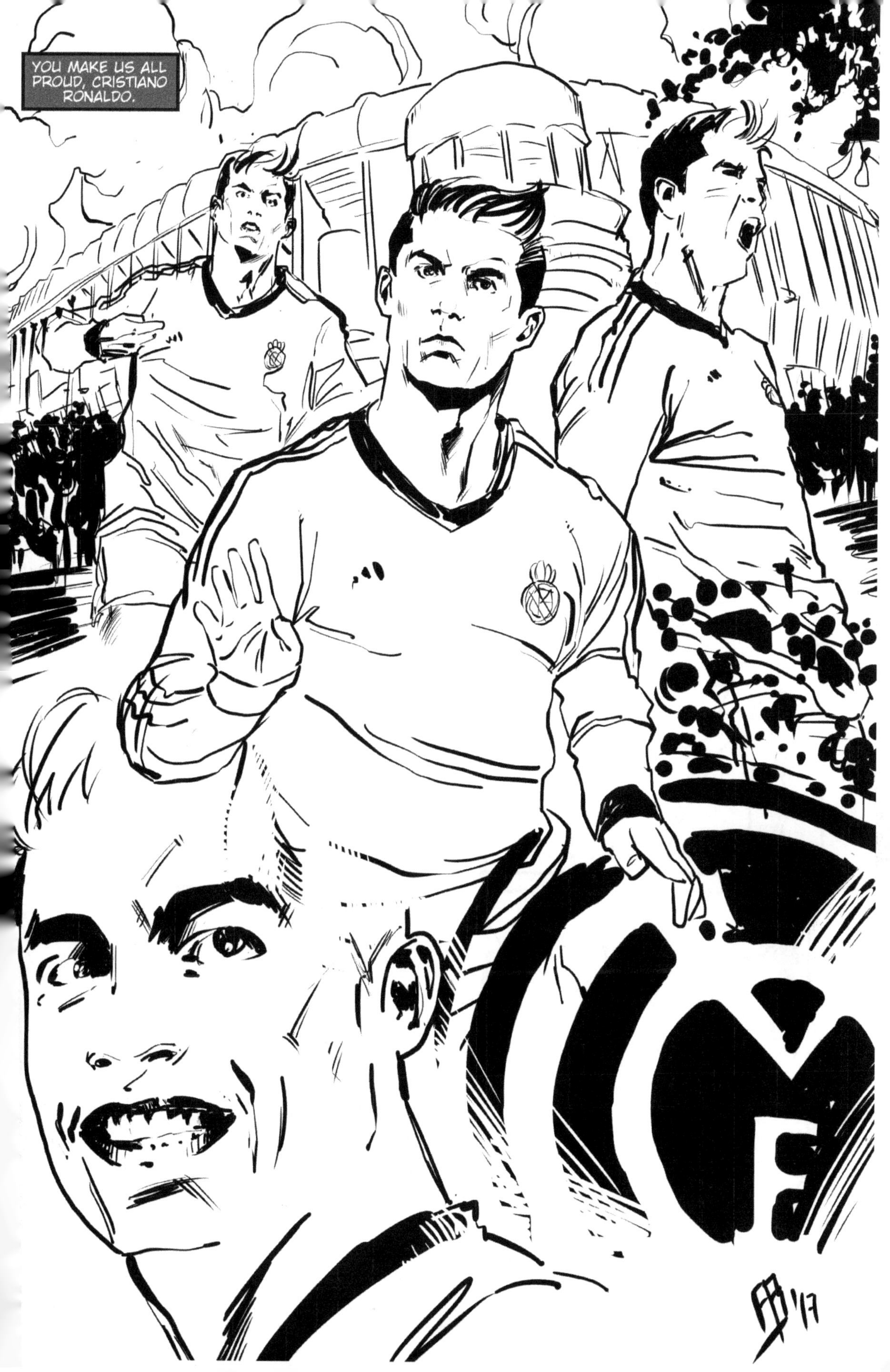
YOU MAKE US ALL PROUD, CRISTIANO RONALDO.

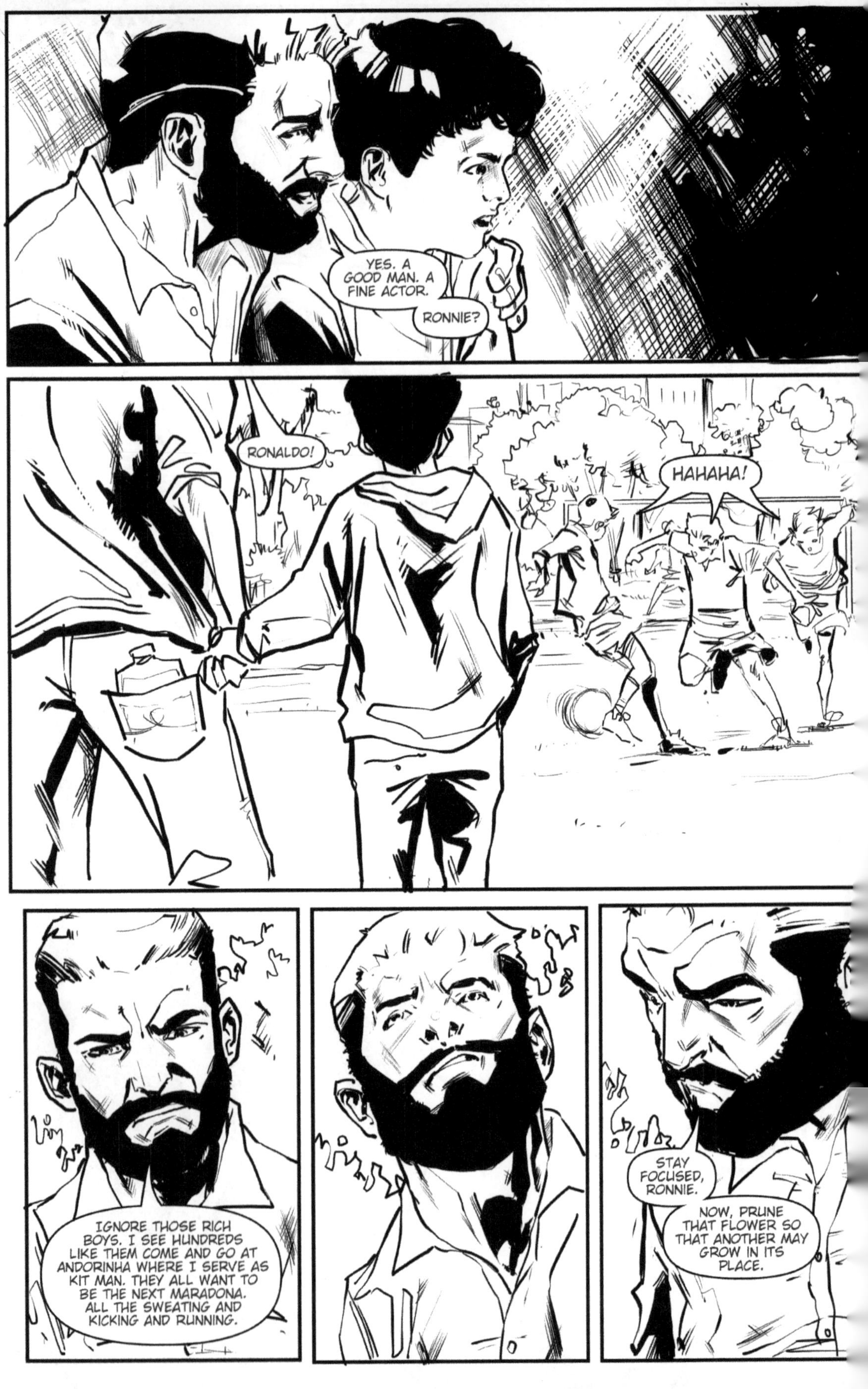
YES. A GOOD MAN. A FINE ACTOR.
RONNIE?
RONALDO!
HAHAHA!
IGNORE THOSE RICH BOYS. I SEE HUNDREDS LIKE THEM COME AND GO AT ANDORINHA WHERE I SERVE AS KIT MAN. THEY ALL WANT TO BE THE NEXT MARADONA. ALL THE SWEATING AND KICKING AND RUNNING.
STAY FOCUSED, RONNIE.
NOW, PRUNE THAT FLOWER SO THAT ANOTHER MAY GROW IN ITS PLACE.

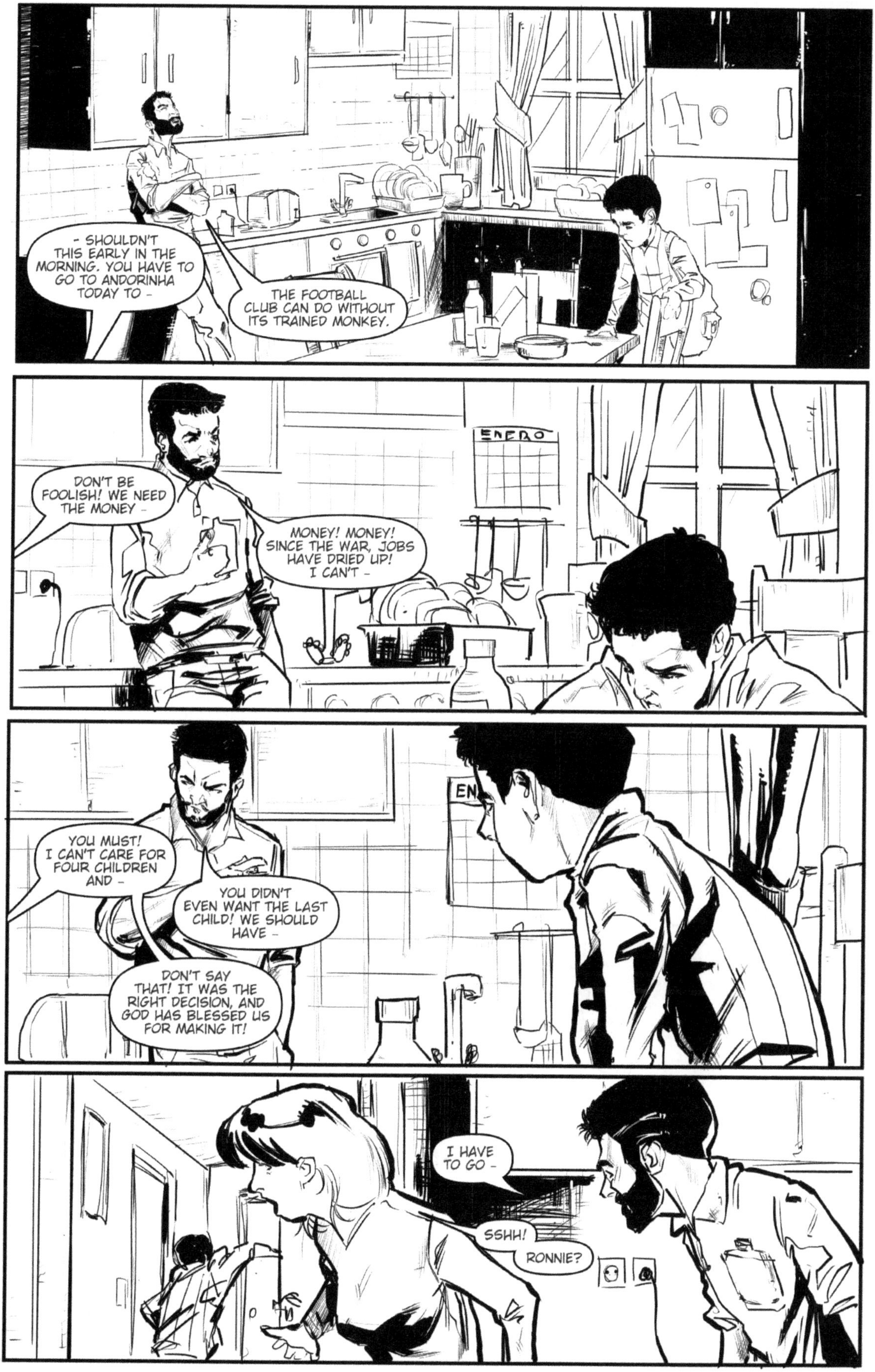
- SHOULDN'T THIS EARLY IN THE MORNING. YOU HAVE TO GO TO ANDORINHA TODAY TO -
THE FOOTBALL CLUB CAN DO WITHOUT ITS TRAINED MONKEY.
ENERO
DON'T BE FOOLISH! WE NEED THE MONEY -
MONEY! MONEY! SINCE THE WAR, JOBS HAVE DRIED UP! I CAN'T -
YOU MUST! I CAN'T CARE FOR FOUR CHILDREN AND -
YOU DIDN'T EVEN WANT THE LAST CHILD! WE SHOULD HAVE -
DON'T SAY THAT! IT WAS THE RIGHT DECISION, AND GOD HAS BLESSED US FOR MAKING IT!
I HAVE TO GO -
SSHH!
RONNIE?

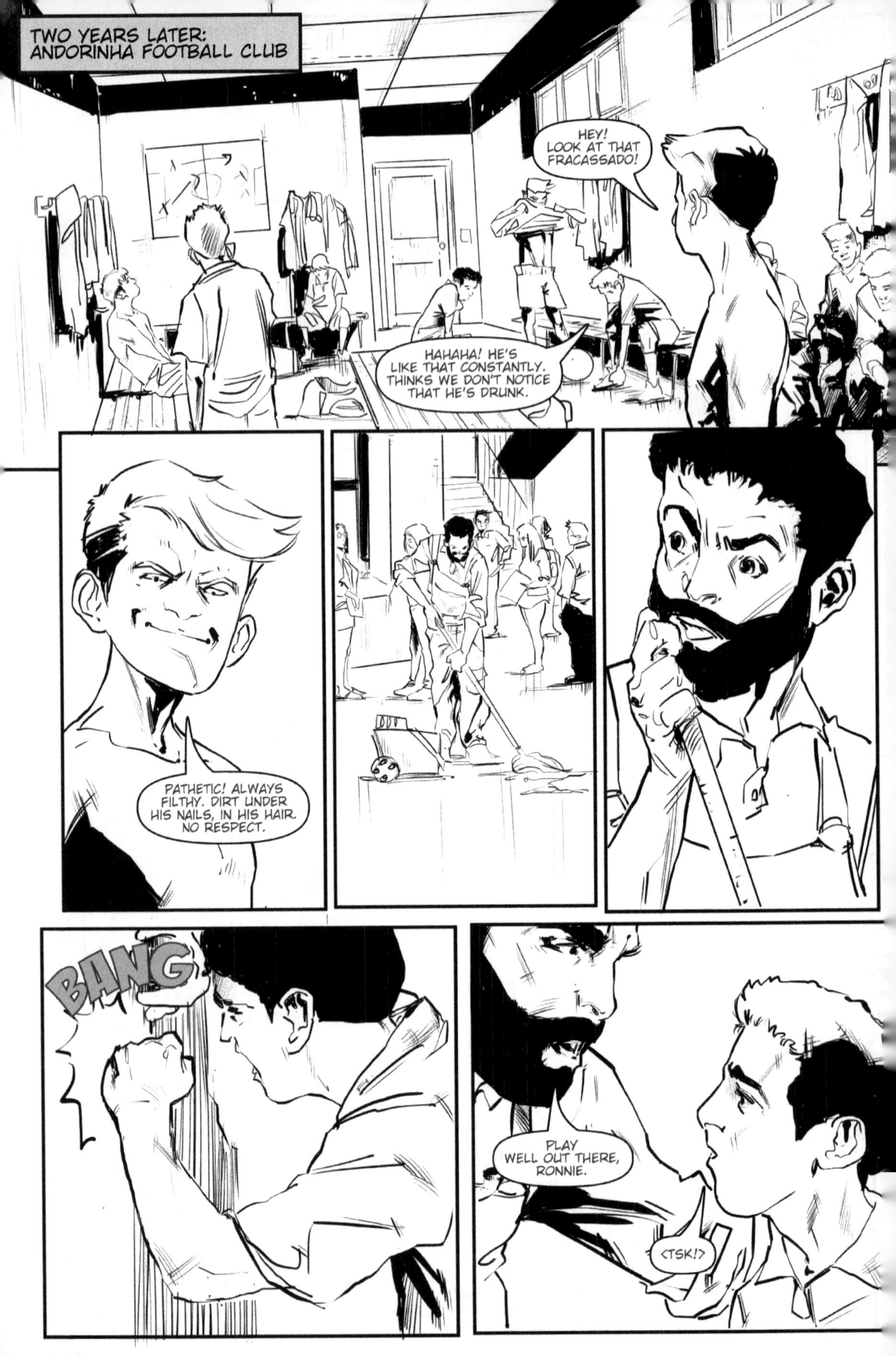
TWO YEARS LATER: ANDORINHA FOOTBALL CLUB
HEY! LOOK AT THAT FRACASSADO!
HAHAHA! HE'S LIKE THAT CONSTANTLY. THINKS WE DON'T NOTICE THAT HE'S DRUNK.
PATHETIC! ALWAYS FILTHY. DIRT UNDER HIS NAILS, IN HIS HAIR. NO RESPECT.
BANG
PLAY WELL OUT THERE, RONNIE.
<TSK!>

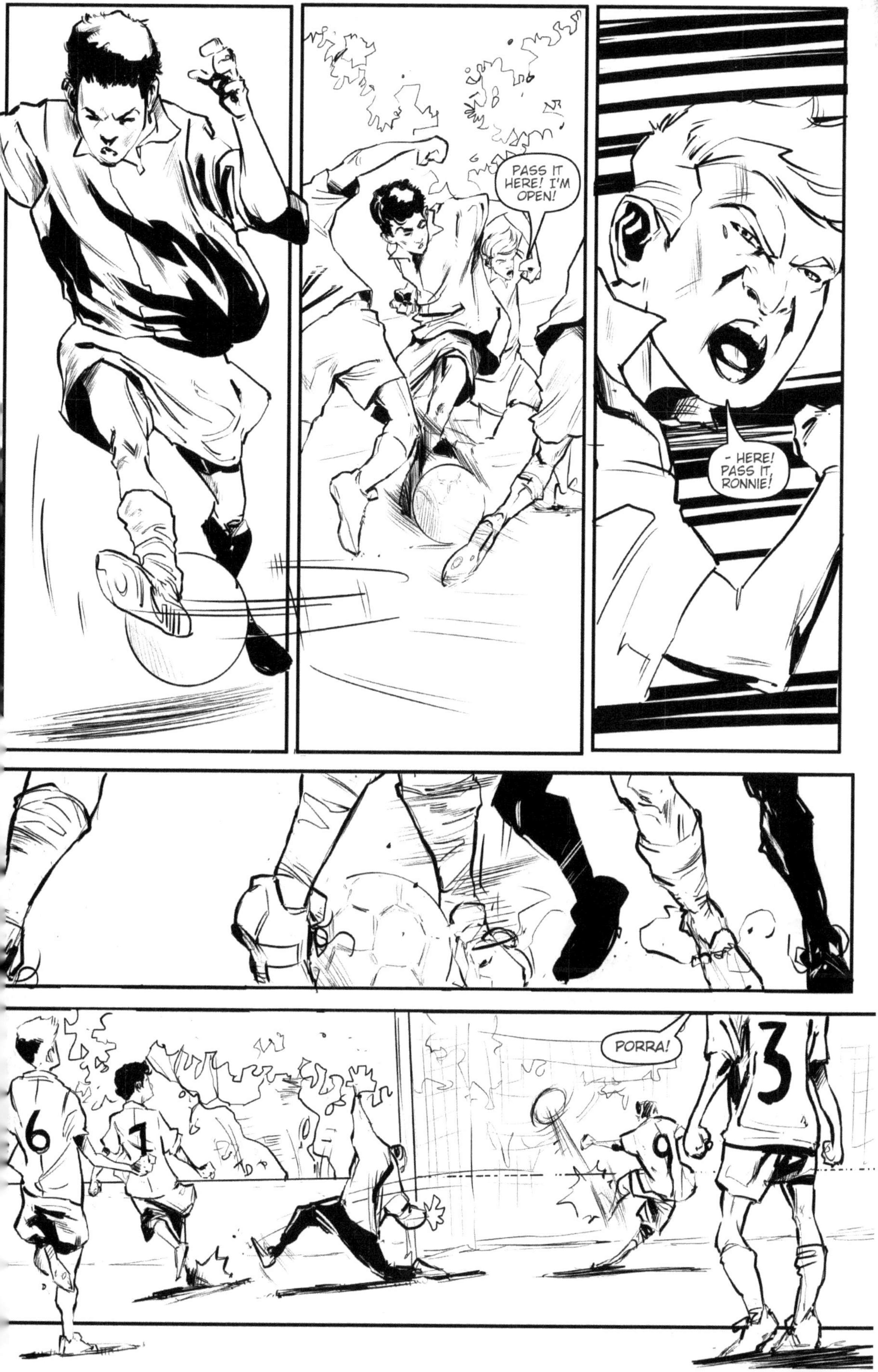
PASS IT HERE! I'M OPEN!
- HERE! PASS IT, RONNIE!
6
7
9
3
PORRA!

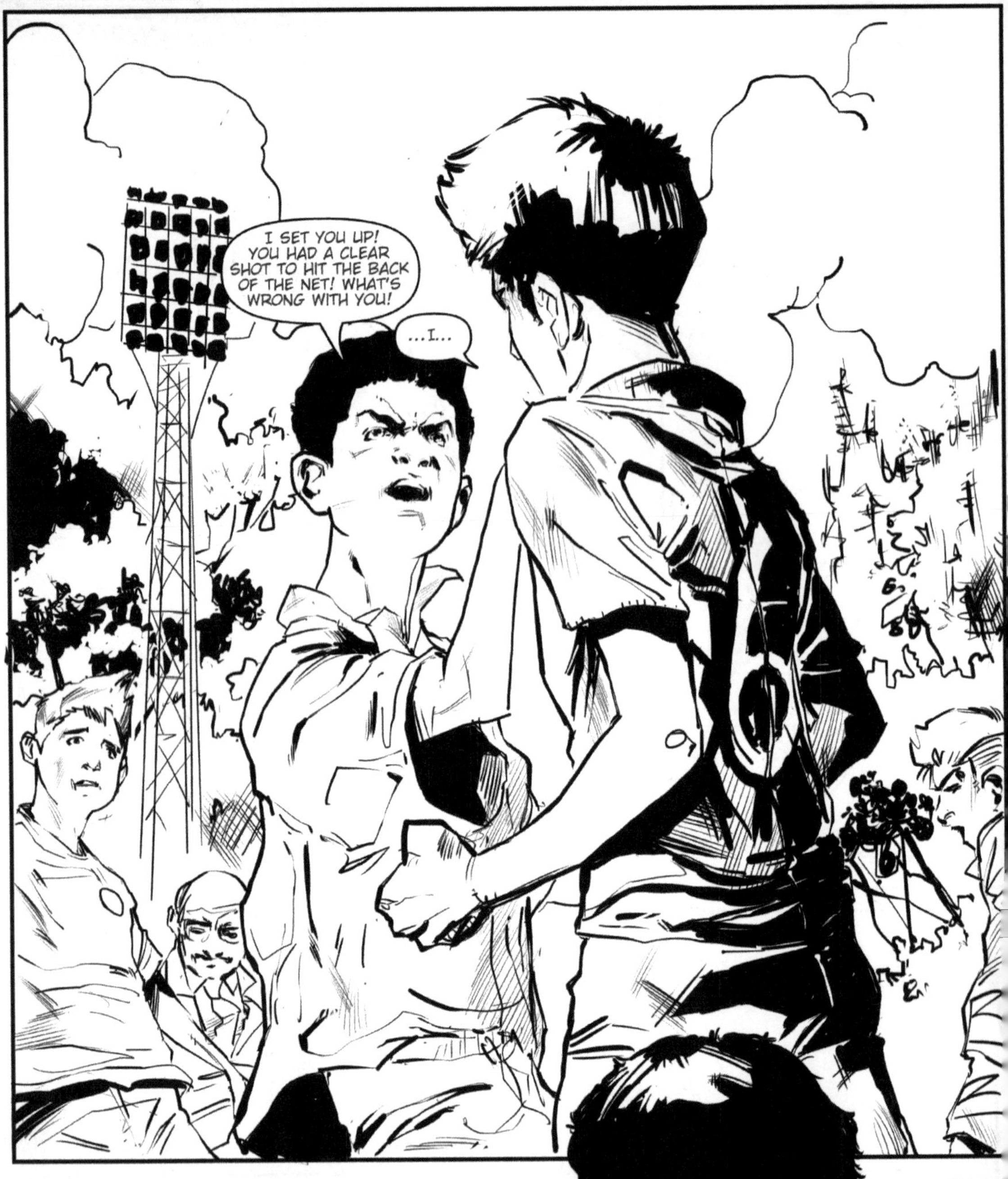
I SET YOU UP! YOU HAD A CLEAR SHOT TO HIT THE BACK OF THE NET! WHAT'S WRONG WITH YOU!
...I...

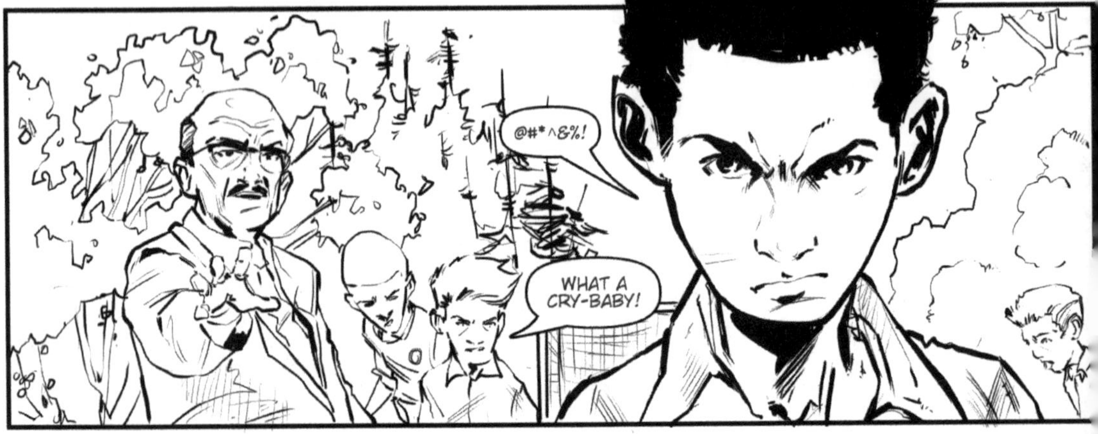
@#*^&%!
WHAT A CRY-BABY!

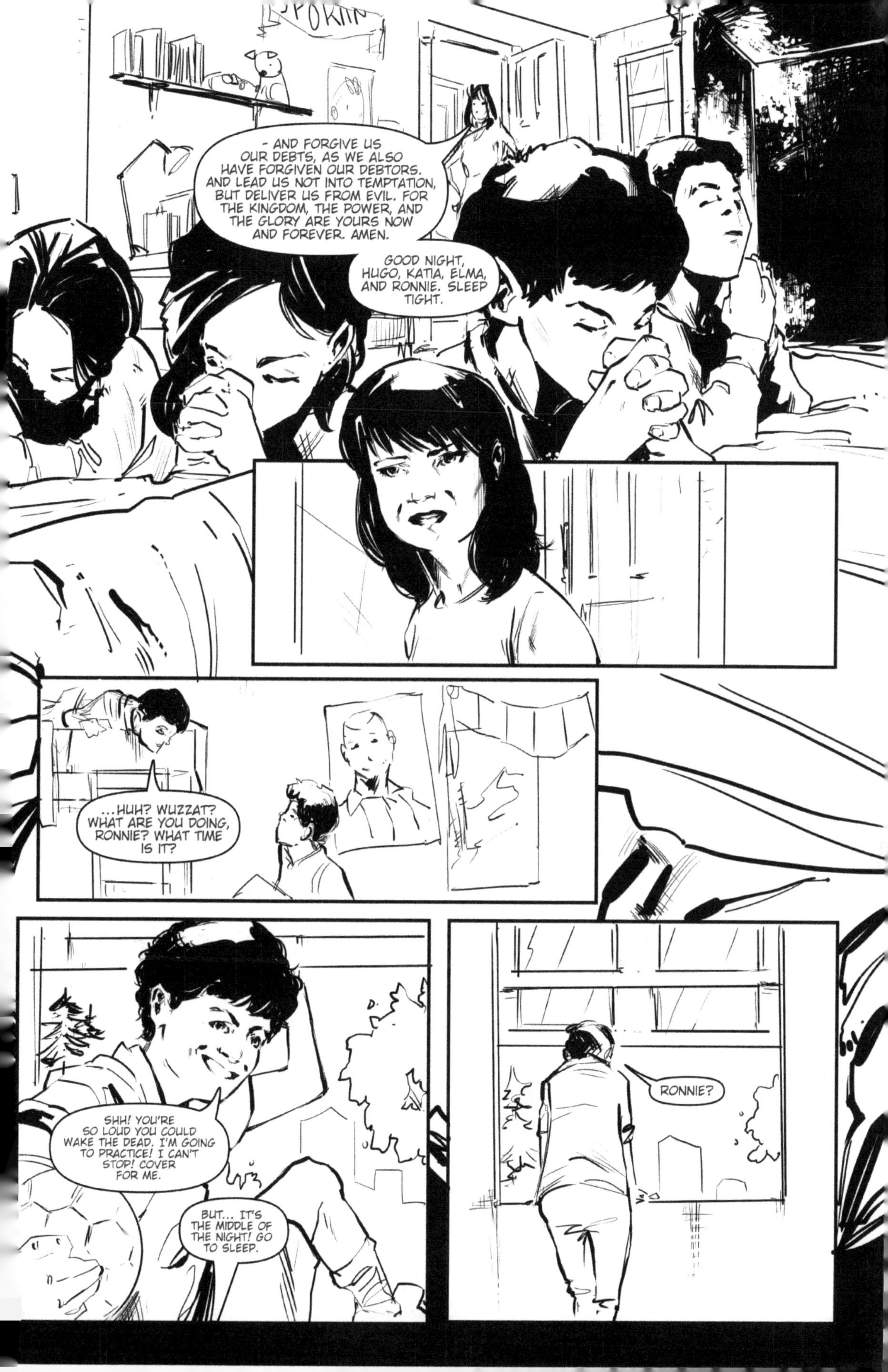
- AND FORGIVE US OUR DEBTS, AS WE ALSO HAVE FORGIVEN OUR DEBTORS. AND LEAD US NOT INTO TEMPTATION, BUT DELIVER US FROM EVIL. FOR THE KINGDOM, THE POWER, AND THE GLORY ARE YOURS NOW AND FOREVER. AMEN.
GOOD NIGHT, HUGO, KATIA, ELMA, AND RONNIE. SLEEP TIGHT.
...HUH? WUZZAT? WHAT ARE YOU DOING, RONNIE? WHAT TIME IS IT?
SHH! YOU'RE SO LOUD YOU COULD WAKE THE DEAD. I'M GOING TO PRACTICE! I CAN'T STOP! COVER FOR ME.
BUT... IT'S THE MIDDLE OF THE NIGHT! GO TO SLEEP.
RONNIE?

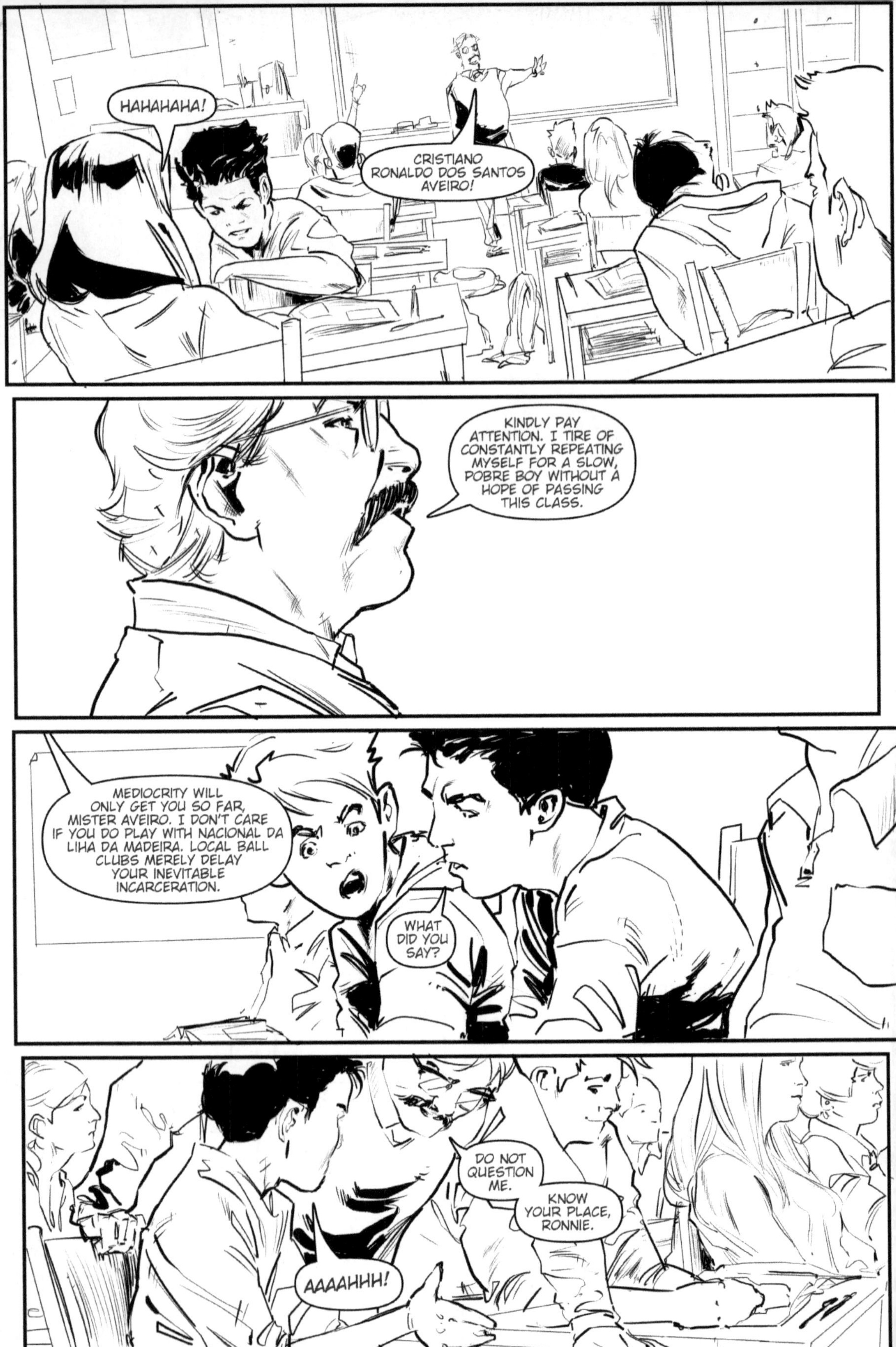
HAHAHAHA!
CRISTIANO RONALDO DOS SANTOS AVEIRO!
KINDLY PAY ATTENTION. I TIRE OF CONSTANTLY REPEATING MYSELF FOR A SLOW, POBRE BOY WITHOUT A HOPE OF PASSING THIS CLASS.
MEDIOCRITY WILL ONLY GET YOU SO FAR, MISTER AVEIRO. I DON'T CARE IF YOU DO PLAY WITH NACIONAL DA LIHA DA MADEIRA. LOCAL BALL CLUBS MERELY DELAY YOUR INEVITABLE INCARCERATION.
WHAT DID YOU SAY?
DO NOT QUESTION ME.
KNOW YOUR PLACE, RONNIE.
AAAAHHH!

TIDALWAVE COMICS

Angel Bernuy & Michael L. Frizell — Writer

Angel Bernuy — Penciler

Darren G. Davis — Editor

Benjamin Glibert — Letterer

Pablo Martinena — Cover

Darren G. Davis
Publisher

Maggie Jessup
Publicity

Susan Ferris
Entertainment Manager

TIDALWAVE PRODUCTIONS

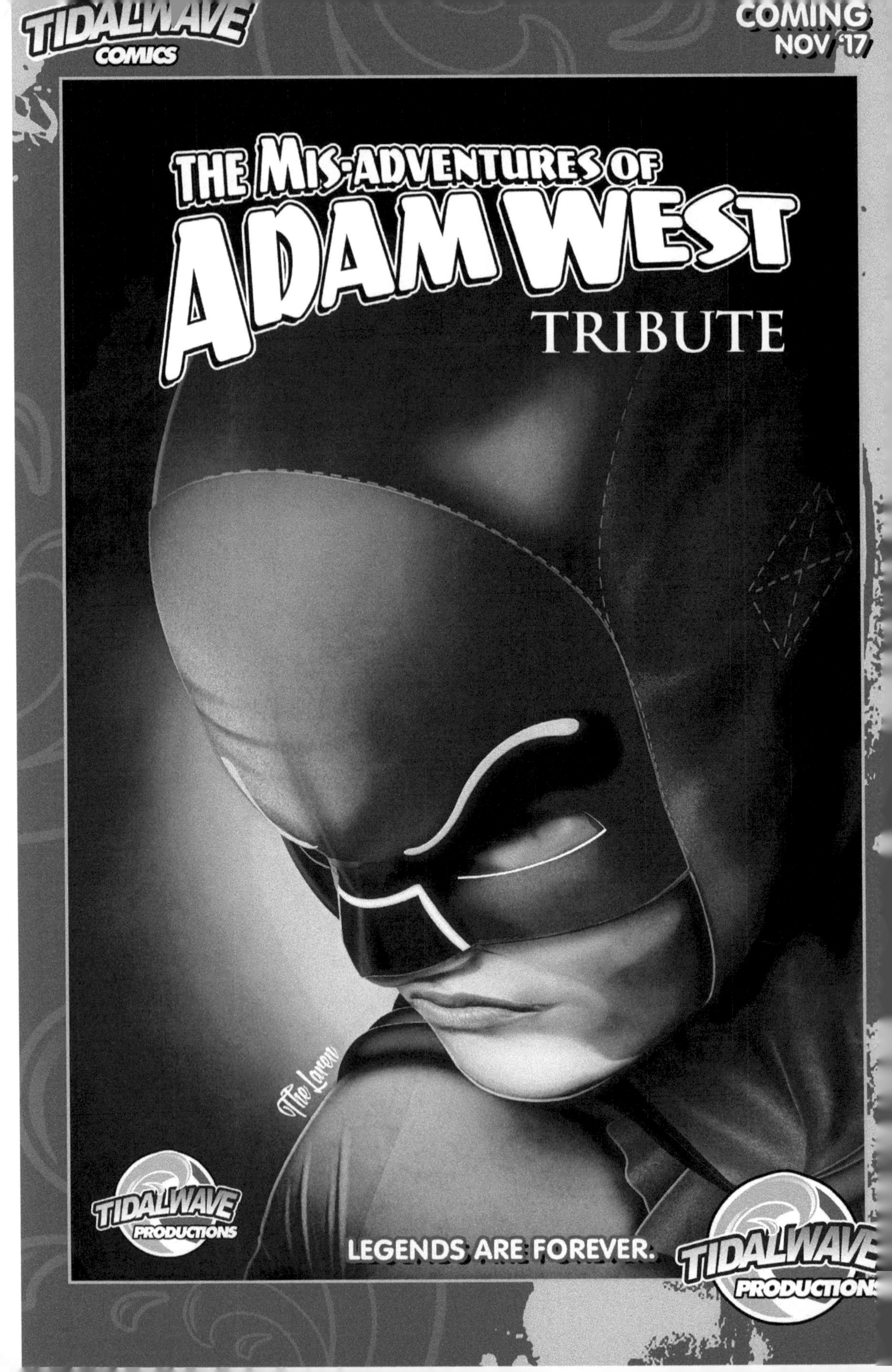
TIDALWAVE COMICS
COMING NOV '17
THE MIS-ADVENTURES OF
ADAM WEST
TRIBUTE
TIDALWAVE PRODUCTIONS
LEGENDS ARE FOREVER.
TIDALWAVE PRODUCTIONS

Lightning Source UK Ltd.
Milton Keynes UK
UKHW051115280919
350575UK00015B/99/P